Verbal Reasoning
Rapid Tests 4

Siân Goodspeed

Schofield & Sims

Introduction

This book gives you practice in answering verbal reasoning questions quickly.

The questions are like the questions on the 11+ and other school selection tests. You must find the correct answers.

School selection tests are usually timed, so you need to get used to working quickly. Each test has a target time for you to work towards. You should time how long you spend on each test, or you can ask an adult to time you.

What you need
- A pencil
- An eraser
- A clock, watch or stopwatch
- A sheet of rough paper
- An adult to help you work out how long you take and to mark the test for you

What to do
- Turn to **Section 1 Test 1** on page 4. Look at the grey box at the top of the page labelled **Target time**. This tells you how long the test should take.
- When you are ready to start, write down the time or start the stopwatch. Or the adult helping you will tell you to begin.
- Find this black arrow ↓ near the top of the first page. Start each test here.
- Find this square ■. The instructions for the first set of questions are beside it. Read them carefully.
- Look below the instructions. Read the **Example**. Work out why the answer given is correct.
- Use a similar method to answer question 1. Show your answer in the way that the answer is shown in the example. For instance, you might need to write your answer on the line or underline the correct answer from a selection given.
- Try to answer every question. If you do get stuck on a question, leave it and go on to the next one. Work quickly and try your best.
- Each test is one page long. When you reach the end, stop. Write down the time or stop the stopwatch. Or tell the adult that you have finished.
- With the adult, work out how long you took to do the test. Fill in the **Time taken** box at the end of the test.
- The adult will mark your test and fill in the **Score** and **Target met?** boxes.
- Turn to the **Progress chart** on page 40. Write your score in the box and colour in the graph to show how many questions you got right.
- Did you get some questions wrong? You should always have another go at them before you look at the answers. Then ask the adult to check your work and help you if you are still not sure.
- Later, you will do some more of these tests. You will soon learn to work through them more quickly. The adult who is helping you will tell you what to do next.

Published by **Schofield & Sims Ltd**,
7 Mariner Court, Wakefield, West Yorkshire WF4 3FL, UK
Telephone 01484 607080
www.schofieldandsims.co.uk
First published in 2014
This edition copyright © Schofield & Sims Ltd, 2018
Seventh impression 2023

Author: **Siân Goodspeed**. Siân Goodspeed has asserted her moral right under the Copyright, Designs and Patents Act, 1988, to be identified as the author of this work.

British Library Cataloguing in Publication Data. A catalogue record for this book is available from the British Library.

All rights reserved. No part of this publication may be reproduced, stored in a retrieval system, or transmitted in any form or by any means, electronic, mechanical, photocopying, recording or otherwise, without either the prior permission of the publisher or a licence permitting restricted copying in the United Kingdom issued by the Copyright Licensing Agency Ltd.

Commissioned by **Carolyn Richardson Publishing Services**
Design by **Oxford Designers & Illustrators**
Front cover design by **Ledgard Jepson Ltd**
Printed in the UK by **Page Bros (Norwich) Ltd**
ISBN 978 07217 1453 0

Contents

Section 1	**Test 1**	Synonyms, Missing three-letter words, Number sequencing, Sorting information	4
	Test 2	Missing numbers, Antonyms, Match the codes, True statements	5
	Test 3	Analogies, Letters for numbers, Letter sequencing, Time problems	6
	Test 4	Antonyms, Missing letters, Letter codes, Maths problems	7
	Test 5	Spot the word, Anagrams, Number connections, Date problems	8
	Test 6	Missing three-letter words, Join two words to make one, Missing numbers, True statements	9
	Test 7	Alphabetical order, Odd ones out, Make a word from two words, Sorting information	10
	Test 8	Synonyms, Word chains, Word codes, Time problems	11
	Test 9	Word connections, Missing numbers, Letter sequencing, Sorting information	12
	Test 10	Odd ones out, Missing three-letter words, Word codes, Complete the word	13
	Test 11	Move a letter, Letters for numbers, Make a word from two words, Maths problems	14
	Test 12	Antonyms, Missing letters, Word codes, Position problems	15
Section 2	**Test 1**	Number sequencing, Join two words to make one, Match the codes, True statements	16
	Test 2	Synonyms, Analogies, Letter sequencing, Date problems	17
	Test 3	Word categories, Letters for numbers, Letter codes, Sorting information	18
	Test 4	Odd ones out, Synonyms, Analogies, Complete the word	19
	Test 5	Number connections, Anagrams, Complete the sentence, Position problems	20
	Test 6	Word chains, Join two words to make one, Alphabetical order, Maths problems	21
	Test 7	Spot the word, Move a letter, Missing letters, Sorting information	22
	Test 8	Antonyms, Missing three-letter words, Complete the sentence, Time problems	23
	Test 9	Move a letter, Odd ones out, Number sequencing, True statements	24
	Test 10	Spot the word, Join two words to make one, Analogies, Date problems	25
	Test 11	Letter sequencing, Missing numbers, Make a new word, Date problems	26
	Test 12	Letter codes, Jumbled sentences, Synonyms, Maths problems	27
Section 3	**Test 1**	Word categories, Spot the word, Word codes, Position problems	28
	Test 2	Number connections, Anagrams, Missing three-letter words, Time problems	29
	Test 3	Move a letter, Missing letters, Match the codes, Complete the word	30
	Test 4	Alphabetical order, Letter codes, Compound words: prefixes, Maths problems	31
	Test 5	Jumbled sentences, Letters for numbers, Letter sequencing, Position problems	32
	Test 6	Synonyms, Alphabetical order, Word codes, Date problems	33
	Test 7	Compound words: prefixes, Missing letters, Spot the word, Time problems	34
	Test 8	Number connections, Antonyms, Word chains, Sorting information	35
	Test 9	Word connections, Analogies, Make a new word, Date problems	36
	Test 10	Letters for numbers, Odd ones out, Letter codes, Maths problems	37
	Test 11	Analogies, Number sequencing, Missing letters, Sorting information	38
	Test 12	Missing numbers, Antonyms, Match the codes, True statements	39

Progress chart   40

A **pull-out answers section** (pages A1 to A8) appears in the centre of this book, between pages 20 and 21. It also gives simple guidance on how best to use this book. Remove this section before the child begins working through the tests.

Section 1 Test 1

Target time: 10 minutes

Underline the two words, **one** from each group, that are most **similar** in meaning.

Example (sent, <u>scent,</u> fascinate)   (fasten, puncture, <u>perfume</u>)

1. (depart, find, devote)   (lose, arrive, leave)
2. (slow, accelerate, halt)   (quicken, race, skid)
3. (pacify, enrage, temper)   (cross, enrich, anger)
4. (museum, ancestor, ancient)   (cousin, old, display)
5. (brawn, power, brave)   (cowardly, electrical, courageous)

In each of the sentences below, the word in capitals has three letters missing. Those three letters spell a word. Write the three-letter word on the line.

Example Sally **M D** the lawn.   ___OWE___   (MOWED)

6. The cows live in the **N**. _____
7. He was **N I N G** for the bus. _____
8. She wrote a **T E R** to her aunt. _____
9. The wet pavement was **S P E R Y**. _____
10. They thought **T** she was guilty. _____

Find the missing number in the sequence. Write it on the line.

Example 32   28   20   16   8   __4__   (repeating pattern −4, −8)

11. 55   40   25   10   ____   −20
12. 1   3   9   27   81   ____
13. 15   18   22   ____   29   32
14. 2.0   ____   3.0   3.5   4.0   4.5

Work out the answers. Write your answers on the lines.

15. Angela is a brown puppy. She has 3 brothers who are black and white, 4 sisters who are brown and 1 sister who is golden. How many brown puppies are there? _____
16. Judy has 3 green marbles, Bethany has 2 yellow marbles and a pink marble and Sandeep has 4 blue marbles. Judy swaps one of her marbles for one of Sandeep's. Bethany swaps one of her yellow marbles for one of Judy's green marbles. What three colours of marble does Judy now have? _____

Score: _____   Time taken: _____   Target met? _____

Section 1 Test 2

Target time: 10 minutes

Find the missing number in each equation. Write the number on the line.

Example 72 + 3 = 25 × ___3___   (72 + 3 = 75 and so does 25 × 3)

1. 80 ÷ 10 = 4 × _____
2. 18 ÷ 6 = 9 ÷ _____
3. 56 ÷ 7 = 5 + _____
4. 10 × 10 = 99 + _____
5. 41 + 2 = 45 − _____

Underline the two words, **one** from each group, that are most **opposite** in meaning.

Example (<u>agitated</u>, tiger, peace)   (<u>calm</u>, vague, eager)

6. (exit, visit, annoy)   (irritate, enter, leave)
7. (super, supper, alike)   (great, awful, awkward)
8. (shop, shelf, sell)   (food, buy, basket)
9. (tiny, tinny, large)   (metal, gigantic, grim)
10. (coward, helpful, hero)   (violent, villain, ally)

Match the number codes to the words. One code is missing. Use these to work out the answers to the questions. Write your answers on the lines.

GOLF   FLOW   WAIT   TALL   8934   4391   7533

11–13. What is the code for: **WALL**? _____ **FLAT**? _____ **GOAL**? _____

14. What does the code **4351** mean? _____

Circle the letter next to the **true** statement for each question.

15. A ruminant is a type of animal that has four stomach chambers. Cows are ruminants.

   If the above statements are true, which one of the following statements must also be true?
   A All ruminants eat grass.
   B Milk comes from cows.
   C Humans are not ruminants.
   D Cows have four stomach chambers.

16. Mushrooms are a kind of fungus. Fungi grow from spores.

   If the above statements are true, which one of the following statements must also be true?
   A All fungi can be eaten.
   B Toadstools are red and white.
   C Mushrooms are poisonous.
   D Mushrooms grow from spores.

Score: _____   Time taken: _____   Target met? _____

Verbal Reasoning Rapid Tests 4

Section 1 Test 3

Target time: 10 minutes

Underline the two words, **one** from each group, that will complete the sentence in the best way.

Example **Detective** is to (inspector, crime, <u>investigate</u>) as **tutor** is to (acrobatics, <u>teach,</u> expect).

1. **Piano** is to (instrument, play, music) as **hammer** is to (noisy, tool, saw).
2. **Nip** is to (nap, pin, bite) as **rat** is to (tail, tar, claws).
3. **Right** is to (wrong, write, up) as **night** is to (evening, knight, nit).
4. **Emerald** is to (sparkly, valuable, green) as **ruby** is to (rogue, red, common).
5. **Snake** is to (creepy, jungle, scales) as **mouse** is to (fur, soft, squeak).

Use the information given to answer the sum. Write your answer as a **letter**.

Example A = 15   B = 29   C = 32   D = 60   E = 8   **D ÷ A × E =** __C__   (60 ÷ 15 × 8 = 32)

6. A = 10   B = 13   C = 4   D = 7   E = 3   **A + E =** _____
7. A = 24   B = 12   C = 2   D = 8   E = 14   **A ÷ C =** _____
8. A = 100   B = 2   C = 50   D = 55   E = 30   **A ÷ B =** _____
9. A = 80   B = 2   C = 140   D = 230   E = 160   **A × B =** _____
10. A = 4   B = 9   C = 96   D = 11   E = 99   **E ÷ B =** _____

Find the missing letter pair in the sequence. Write it on the line. You might need to use a different method from the example given. Use the alphabet to help you.

A B C D E F G H I J K L M N O P Q R S T U V W X Y Z

Example   JP   ML   PH   SD   VZ   __YV__   (+3, −4)

11. DB   MB   EB   NB   _____   OB   GB   13. AZ   BW   CT   DQ   _____   FK
12. UM   DJ   VN   EK   WO   FL   _____   14. BP   DN   FL   HJ   _____   LF   ND

Work out the answers. Write your answers on the lines.

15. Janice is finishing work at 17:00. It takes her 40 minutes to travel home. Her husband is preparing dinner ready for her arrival. It will take him 1 hour and 35 minutes to cook dinner. What time does he need to begin cooking to make sure that Janice's meal is ready for her when she gets home? _____

16. Deshi composes a song that is 2 minutes and 15 seconds long. It has two verses and one chorus. Each verse lasts 50 seconds. How many seconds does the chorus last? _____

Score: _____   Time taken: _____   Target met? _____

Section 1 Test 4

Target time: 10 minutes

Underline the pair of words that are most **opposite** in meaning.

Example (<u>agitated, calm</u>)   (peace, vague)   (tiger, eager)

1. (weight, wait)   (slow, big)   (heavy, light)
2. (ticket, price)   (answer, question)   (exam, paper)
3. (shore, island)   (slow, rapid)   (river, lake)
4. (sweet, bitter)   (lemon, silky)   (gently, beastly)
5. (unsure, allowed)   (double, detailed)   (certain, doubtful)

Find **one** missing letter that completes **both** pairs of words. Write it on the lines.

Example tre [_e_] asy   lik [_e_] ver   (tree and easy, like and ever)

6. iro [__] ever   spi [__] ear
7. col [__] eaf   re [__] one
8. cal [__] ore   broo [__] eet
9. driv [__] xit   bruis [__] xpect
10. staf [__] orget   puf [__] loat

Using the alphabet to help you, find the letters that complete each sentence. Write the letters on the line.

A B C D E F G H I J K L M N O P Q R S T U V W X Y Z

Example JB is to PY as KR is to __QO__.   (+6, −3)

11. JP is to FL as VI is to _____.
12. KQ is to NT as EO is to _____.
13. GU is to BP as MY is to _____.
14. MF is to OI as VP is to _____.

Work out the answers. Write your answers on the lines.

15. Leena is a chef. Her restaurant serves two special meals a night. They are listed on the specials menu. Tonight Leena receives 34 orders for Special One and 45 orders for Special Two. Everybody else who eats in the restaurant orders from the usual menu, not the specials menu. Altogether, Leena receives 200 food orders. How many people order from the usual menu? _____

16. Gary wants to print his science project. He goes to the shop to buy paper. His project is 4000 pages long. The shop sells paper in boxes of 900 sheets. What is the lowest number of boxes of paper Gary must buy to print his project? _____

Score:	Time taken:	Target met?

Section 1 Test 5

Target time: 10 minutes

Find the **four-letter word** hidden across two or more consecutive words in each sentence below. The order of the letters must stay the same. Underline the word and write it on the line.

Example You certainly <u>do l</u>ead an interesting life. _____dole_____

1. How is his dog? _____
2. Her train was the last arrival. _____
3. Parachutists jump out of planes. _____
4. My uncle answered the phone. _____
5. Which one is yours? _____

Underline the **two** words that contain all the same letters.

Example plan   <u>lamp</u>   lame   <u>palm</u>   pale

6. pore   role   poke   rope   roar
7. pair   pale   leap   pile   lean
8. lope   pole   loan   pore   loam
9. line   mire   mile   mine   lime
10. vote   save   toes   sate   vase

Work out the missing number and write it on the line.

Example 36 [6] 6   45 [9] 5   25 [__5__] 5
(a ÷ b = ?, where a represents the number on the left and b represents the number on the right)

11. 9 [45] 5   12 [144] 12   9 [_____] 9
12. 24 [8] 3   3 [1] 3   77 [_____] 7
13. 63 [21] 3   100 [20] 5   1 [_____] 1
14. 250 [100] 150   310 [140] 170   85 [_____] 40

Work out the answers. Write your answers on the lines.

15. Stacey is 5 years older than her sister Macey who is 6 years old. How old is Stacey? _____

16. It was Tuesday 3 days ago. What day is it today? _____

Score: _____   Time taken: _____   Target met? _____

Section 1 Test 6

Target time: 10 minutes

In each of the sentences below, the word in capitals has three letters missing. Those three letters spell a word. Write the three-letter word on the line.

Example Sally **M D** the lawn.   ___OWE___   (MOWED)

1. She bought a new **P** of shoes.   _____
2. His car had **N** stolen.   _____
3. The football game **I N S** at 10 o'clock.   _____
4. The **E** was lit by matches.   _____
5. I washed my hands with soap and hot **W R**.   _____

Underline the two words, **one** from each group, that together make one new word. The word from the first group comes first.

Example (<u>kit</u>, pip, nine)   (comic, <u>ten</u>, numb)   (kitten)

6. (films, camera, view)   (planet, star, point)
7. (bag, neck, paper)   (lace, fabric, sewing)
8. (paper, box, file)   (sign, clip, office)
9. (fair, unjust, bad)   (ground, play, good)
10. (help, aid, mist)   (gift, line, row)

Find the missing number in each equation. Write the number on the line.

Example 72 + 3 = 25 × ___3___   (72 + 3 = 75 and so does 25 × 3)

11. 84 − 4 = 8 × _____
12. 50 ÷ 2 = 5 × _____
13. 99 ÷ 9 = 17 − 3 − _____
14. 20 × 3 = 64 − _____

Circle the letter next to the **true** statement for each question.

15. People who travel on aeroplanes are called passengers. Li is going to London on an aeroplane.

    If the above statements are true, which one of the following statements must also be true?
    - **A** All aeroplanes fly to London.
    - **B** Li is a passenger.
    - **C** People on trains are called travellers.
    - **D** Li will take a taxi to her hotel.

16. Where an animal lives is called its habitat. A badger's habitat is called a sett.

    If the above statements are true, which one of the following statements must also be true?
    - **A** Badgers live in setts.
    - **B** Foxes and badgers live in the countryside.
    - **C** Badgers have black and white stripes.
    - **D** Badgers are hairy animals.

Score: _____   Time taken: _____   Target met? _____

Verbal Reasoning Rapid Tests 4

Section 1 Test 7

Target time: 10 minutes

If these words were listed in alphabetical order, which word would come **third**? Write the answer on the line.

Example kite colourful breeze blow chase   ____chase____

1. car   bike   train   tram   walk   _____
2. clock   tick   turn   time   chime   _____
3. mouse   scrabble   squeak   cheese   scratch   _____
4. book   read   line   word   writing   _____
5. brain   heart   wrist   head   back   _____

In each group, three words go together and two are the odd ones out. Underline the **two** words that do **not** go with the other three.

Example scalding, sweltering, bitter, raw, roasting

6. under, over, always, out, never
7. pelican, ferret, hamster, flamingo, toucan
8. cottage, maisonette, office, mansion, barn
9. maracas, quiver, violin, chain, flute
10. rectangle, cube, circle, pyramid, sphere

The word in square brackets has been made by some of the letters from the two outside words. Make a new word in the middle of the second group of words in the same way. Write the new word on the line.

Example (scope [soap] adder)   (warns [__wren__] elder)

11. (huge [hunt] note)   (sing [_____] gone)   13. (luck [bulk] cube)   (iron [_____] wigs)
12. (hope [pith] bite)   (neck [_____] boil)   14. (seal [eels] pear)   (kiln [_____] owed)

Work out the answers. Write your answers on the lines.

15. Three friends share a pepperoni pizza and a cheese pizza. Each pizza is cut into 6 slices. They divide the pizza so that they all have the same amount. Brin doesn't like pepperoni pizza, but Iwona likes both flavours. If Brin doesn't eat any pepperoni pizza and Steph only eats pepperoni pizza, how many slices of cheese pizza does Iwona eat? _____

16. A farmer has 3 cows and 7 goats. He has twice as many chickens as he has goats. He has three times as many ducks as he has cows. The number of cats he has is one-fifth of 25. How many animals does the farmer have altogether? _____

Score: Time taken: Target met?

Section 1 Test 8

Target time: 10 minutes

Underline the two words, **one** from each group, that are most **similar** in meaning.

Example (sent, <u>scent</u>, fascinate)   (fasten, puncture, <u>perfume</u>)

1. (rock, shake, cradle)   (quiver, arrow, target)
2. (blame, detain, embrace)   (refer, lame, hug)
3. (blind, peak, peek)   (addition, deaf, summit)
4. (real, roll, reel)   (genuine, false, trust)
5. (livid, kidney, lilac)   (lung, furious, exist)

Change the first word into the last word by changing only **one** letter at a time, making a new word in the middle. Write the new word on the line.

Example LAKE [__LANE__] PANE

6. GLUE [_____] BLUB
7. WINK [_____] PUNK
8. BOAT [_____] MOST
9. WILD [_____] MILK
10. LOVE [_____] LONG

Using the alphabet to help you, crack the code. Write your answer on the line.

A B C D E F G H I J K L M N O P Q R S T U V W X Y Z

Example If the code for **TALK** is **GZOP**, what is the code for **LOUD**?   __OLFW__
(mirror code – each letter is the same distance from the opposite end of the alphabet)

11. If the code for **BED** is **YVW**, what is the code for **LED**? _____
12. If the code for **AID** is **ZRW**, what is the code for **EAT**? _____
13. If the code for **YES** is **BVH**, what is the code for **HIT**? _____
14. If **GOT** is written in code as **TLG**, what is the code for **MAN**? _____

Work out the answers. Write your answers on the lines.

15. A ballet performance will begin at 19:00. It will be performed in two halves with a 20-minute break between the first and second half. Each half will be 50 minutes long. What time will the ballet performance end? _____

16. Kingsley's watch is set 10 minutes slow. Mary knows that her watch is running slow but she isn't sure how slow. Kingsley's watch says that the time is 10.20 a.m. Mary's watch says it is 10.05 a.m. How many minutes behind the real time is Mary's watch? _____

Score:	Time taken:	Target met?

Verbal Reasoning Rapid Tests 4

Section 1 Test 9

Target time: 10 minutes

Underline the word that goes best with the three words in brackets.

Example (paint, chalk, pastel) <u>ink</u>, sketch, colour

1. (mint, chocolate, strawberry) vanilla, pastel, ice cream
2. (sigh, breathe, exhale) stretch, faint, wheeze
3. (vile, disgusting, repulsive) revolting, attractive, masked
4. (ramble, mutter, stammer) trek, stumble, murmur
5. (dent, damage, scuff) flail, scrape, replace

Find the missing number in each equation. Write the number on the line.

Example 72 + 3 = 25 × __3__ (72 + 3 = 75 and so does 25 × 3)

6. 200 − 90 = 10 × _____ + 10
7. 144 ÷ 12 = 15 − _____
8. 25 × 5 = 120 + 3 + _____
9. 22 + 88 = 130 − 21 + _____
10. 59 − 3 = 8 × _____ − 8

Find the missing letter pair in the sequence. Write it on the line. Use the alphabet to help you.

A B C D E F G H I J K L M N O P Q R S T U V W X Y Z

Example JP ML PH SD VZ __YV__ (+3, −4)

11. NK ZG OL YH _____ XI QN
12. OH PI _____ RK SL TM UN
13. FP ZZ EO AA DN BB _____
14. GB ID KF _____ OJ QL SN

Work out the answers. Write your answers on the lines.

15. Zara is wearing a necklace and a ring. Alicia is wearing a ring, a bracelet and a necklace. Lia is wearing a bracelet. All of the girls' jewellery is gold, except for Alicia's ring which is silver. How many girls are wearing gold necklaces? _____

16. Michael and Fatima drink tea with milk. Husna likes her tea with milk and two sugars. Angela has her tea the same way as Fatima. Delia drinks coffee with no milk and one sugar. Delia's daughter prefers lemonade to tea or coffee. How many people take milk with their drink? _____

Score: _____ Time taken: _____ Target met? _____

Section 1 Test 10

Target time: 10 minutes

In each group, three words go together and two are the odd ones out. Underline the **two** words that do **not** go with the other three.

Example scalding, sweltering, bitter, raw, roasting

1. pliers, spatula, spanner, whisk, grater
2. screwdriver, banner, flag, hammer, spanner
3. decrease, reduce, raise, lift, elevate
4. hot, frozen, warm, cold, tepid
5. joyful, miserable, pleased, sad, happy

In each of the sentences below, the word in capitals has three letters missing. Those three letters spell a word. Write the three-letter word on the line.

Example Sally **M D** the lawn.   O W E   (MOWED)

6. The **SOR** climbed aboard the ship. _____
7. Their **MARRI** was very happy. _____
8. The letter was **IMPORT**. _____
9. Without my friends I felt **LLY**. _____
10. Throwing the food away seemed like a **TE**. _____

Using the alphabet to help you, crack the code. Write your answer on the line.

A B C D E F G H I J K L M N O P Q R S T U V W X Y Z

Example If the code for **CART** is **EZTS**, what is the code for **KING**?   MHPF   (+2, −1, +2, −1)

11. If the code for **TABLE** is **UCEPJ**, what is the code for **MUG**? _____
12. If the code for **FEET** is **KJJY**, what is the code for **ROPE**? _____
13. If **STRAW** is written in code as **RRQYV**, what does the code **RYLC** mean? _____
14. If **BLACK** is written in code as **AJZAJ**, what is the code for **WHITE**? _____

Some letters are missing from the words below. Use the word's definition to help you fill in the missing letters. Write the word on the line.

Example G __ __ E __ __ US   giving, charitable   GENEROUS

15. AS __ O __ IS __ ED   surprised, amazed, astounded _____
16. IN __ __ L __ IG __ NT   clever, brainy, smart _____

Section 1 Test 11

Target time: 10 minutes

Move one letter from the first word to the second word to make two new words. Do not reorder the letters. Write the two new words on the lines.

Example spray, eat   _____pray_____ , _____seat_____   (move the s)

1. cram, old   _____ , _____
2. driver, ripping   _____ , _____
3. beard, done   _____ , _____
4. bird, though   _____ , _____
5. glow, ban   _____ , _____

Use the information given to answer the sum. Write your answer as a **letter**.

Example A = 15   B = 29   C = 32   D = 60   E = 8   D ÷ A × E = __C__   (60 ÷ 15 × 8 = 32)

6. A = 10   B = 4   C = 21   D = 7   E = 2   (A + B) ÷ E = _____
7. A = 20   B = 2   C = 1   D = 11   E = 34   (A + B) ÷ D = _____
8. A = 9   B = 100   C = 10   D = 5   E = 50   (E − D) ÷ D = _____
9. A = 172   B = 3   C = 2   D = 10   E = 17   (A − C) ÷ D = _____
10. A = 9   B = 13   C = 12   D = 11   E = 32   A + D + C = _____

The word in square brackets has been made by some of the letters from the two outside words. Make a new word in the middle of the second group of words in the same way. Write the new word on the line.

Example (scope [soap] adder)   (warns [__wren__] elder)

11. (long [hold] dash) (city [_____] exam)
12. (claw [crow] roam) (font [_____] isle)
13. (lace [call] legs) (dare [_____] idle)
14. (fire [fend] dent) (fool [_____] glow)

Work out the answers. Write your answers on the lines.

15. Jack has 3 cookies. Sam has 5 more than Jack. Susan has half the number Sam has. How many cookies does Susan have? _____

16. There are 14 balloons in a bunch. Will takes 7, Zoë takes 1 and Habib takes 4. Jenny takes the rest. How many balloons does Jenny have? _____

Score: _____   Time taken: _____   Target met? _____

14   Schofield & Sims

Section 1 Test 12

Target time: 10 minutes

Underline the word in brackets that is most **opposite** in meaning to the word in capitals.

Example AGITATED (tiger, calm, vague, eager, peace)

1. SUCCESS (trespass, injure, survive, failure, promote)
2. STALE (sty, baked, fresh, breathe, exhale)
3. SAVE (traipse, spend, expel, suspend, confer)
4. FORGET (memories, explain, imagine, consider, remember)
5. GUILTY (gullible, innocent, incense, forgive, evil)

Find **one** missing letter that completes **both** pairs of words. Write it on the lines.

Example tre [e] asy   lik [e] ver   (tree and easy, like and ever)

6. chi [__] ine   throw [__] earby
7. pani [__] homp   traffi [__] one
8. bandi [__] rain   por [__] read
9. boar [__] elight   plo [__] ear
10. sno [__] eek   cla [__] rong

Using the alphabet to help you, crack the code. Write your answer on the line.

A B C D E F G H I J K L M N O P Q R S T U V W X Y Z

Example If the code for **TALK** is **GZOP**, what is the code for **LOUD**? __OLFW__
(mirror code – each letter is the same distance from the opposite end of the alphabet)

11. If **NEED** is written in code as **MVVW**, what is the code for **BOAT**? _____
12. If the code for **SOFA** is **HLUZ**, what is the code for **CHAIR**? _____
13. If the code for **BOOK** is **YLLP**, what is the code for **MARK**? _____
14. If **KZTV** means **PAGE**, what does the code **OVGGVI** mean? _____

Work out the answers. Write your answers on the lines.

15. There were seven people in a queue. Molly was in the lead with Charlie behind her. Samuel was at the back with Paul in front of him. Paul was behind Lilian, who was behind Shahzeb. Amelia was behind Charlie. Who was third in the queue? _____

16. Four people had a race. Georgiana won and John came second. Jason, who was just beaten by Lewis, came last. Who finished third? _____

Score: ____   Time taken: ____   Target met? ____

Verbal Reasoning Rapid Tests 4

Section 2 Test 1

Target time: 10 minutes

Find the missing number in the sequence. Write it on the line.

Example 32   28   20   16   8   __4__   (repeating pattern −4, −8)

1. 1   2   6   12   36   _____   216
2. 7   18   14   36   28   _____   56
3. 88   76   64   52   _____   28   16
4. _____   2000   1000   500   250
5. 8.00   8.25   8.50   8.75   9.00   _____

Underline the two words, **one** from each group, that together make one new word. The word from the first group comes first.

Example (<u>kit</u>, pip, nine)   (comic, <u>ten</u>, numb)   (kitten)

6. (so, sew, see)   (weed, lid, not)
7. (she, he, it)   (eat, art, ink)
8. (is, his, isle)   (sand, land, place)
9. (fire, match, flame)   (plot, place, area)
10. (net, catch, fish)   (bounce, ball, throw)

Match the number codes to the words. One code is missing. Use these to work out the answers to the questions. Write your answers on the lines.

SELL   LEAP   SALE   BARE   9155   4281   5123

11–13. What is the code for: **PALE**? _____   **PEAR**? _____   **BELL**? _____

14. What does the code **9 5 1 1 3** mean? _____

Circle the letter next to the **true** statement for each question.

15. Gemstones are made from minerals. Diamonds are a type of gemstone.

    If the above statements are true, which one of the following statements must also be true?
    A Gemstones are very shiny.
    B Diamonds are used for jewellery.
    C Diamonds are made from minerals.
    D Minerals are beautiful.

16. Locomotives travel on railway lines. Trains are pulled by locomotives.

    If the above statements are true, which one of the following statements must also be true?
    A Trains use railway lines.
    B The Tube is in London.
    C Some trains travel through tunnels.
    D Trains are very long.

Score: _____   Time taken: _____   Target met? _____

Section 2 Test 2

Target time: 10 minutes

Underline the word in brackets that is **closest** in meaning to the word in capitals.

Example SCENT (puncture, perfume, sent, fascinate)

1. CHANGE (cellar, alter, penny, dress, cheat)
2. TUNE (salmon, boast, satchel, explain, melody)
3. STOP (start, oceans, cease, season, waves)
4. SKILL (dance, skeleton, tap, talent, bend)
5. ABLE (mutter, complain, capable, mumble, cursed)

Underline the two words, **one** from each group, that will complete the sentence in the best way.

Example **Detective** is to (inspector, crime, investigate) as **tutor** is to (acrobatics, teach, expect).

6. **Bull** is to (charge, horns, Spain) as **deer** is to (antlers, hooves, tusks).
7. **Desert** is to (sandy, dry, scorching) as **arctic** is to (freezing, mild, snow).
8. **Tyre** is to (rubber, circle, spin) as **windscreen** is to (transparent, glass, view).
9. **Nurse** is to (uniform, hospital, caring) as **teacher** is to (exam, timetable, school).
10. **Uncle** is to (aunt, nephew, brother) as **mother** is to (nanny, father, carer).

Find the missing letter pair in the sequence. Write it on the line. Use the alphabet to help you.

A B C D E F G H I J K L M N O P Q R S T U V W X Y Z

Example JP ML PH SD VZ __YV__ (+3, −4)

11. LZ GQ MZ HR NZ IS _____
12. WJ XR YJ _____ AJ BR
13. MS NO OK PG _____ RY
14. TA PH _____ QI VC RJ WD

Work out the answers. Write your answers on the lines.

15. How many days after 3 June is 25 June? _____
16. What will the date be a fortnight after 6 September? _____

Score: Time taken: Target met?

Verbal Reasoning Rapid Tests 4

Section 2 Test 3

Target time: 10 minutes

1–5. Look at the words in groups A, B and C. For each of the words below, choose the correct group and write its letter on the line.

A	B	C
basketball	ice-skating	diving

skiing _____   windsurfing _____   football _____   snowboarding _____   swimming _____
snorkelling _____   netball _____   toboganning _____   rugby _____   rafting _____

Use the information given to answer the sum. Write your answer as a **letter**.

Example A = 15   B = 29   C = 32   D = 60   E = 8   **D ÷ A × E =** __C__   (60 ÷ 15 × 8 = 32)

6. A = 12   B = 2   C = 36   D = 6   E = 0   **A ÷ B × E =** _____
7. A = 10   B = 5   C = 2   D = 25   E = 35   **A ÷ C × B =** _____
8. A = 16   B = 8   C = 2   D = 14   E = 32   **B × C × C =** _____
9. A = 10   B = 12   C = 2   D = 100   E = 140 **(B − C) × A =** _____
10. A = 9   B = 5   C = 400   D = 10   E = 450 **B × A × D =** _____

Using the alphabet to help you, find the letters that complete each sentence. Write the letters on the line. You might need to use a different method from the example given.

A B C D E F G H I J K L M N O P Q R S T U V W X Y Z

Example **JB** is to **PY** as **KR** is to __QO__.   (+6, −3)

11. **QK** is to **NI** as **JU** is to _____.   13. **TR** is to **PP** as **XK** is to _____.
12. **CE** is to **XV** as **DB** is to _____.   14. **SG** is to **XJ** as **DQ** is to _____.

Work out the answers. Write your answers on the lines.

15. Harry and Dylan finish school at 3.00 p.m. Emma usually finishes school at 4.15 p.m. but today she has a detention until 5.00 p.m. Ginny finishes lessons at 4.20 p.m. Angel and Dan finish school at 4.10 p.m. It takes all the children 10 minutes to walk home from school. How many of the children will be at home by 4.30 p.m.? _____

16. Anna is going to a fancy dress party. When Anna arrives at the party there are already 15 other people there. A third of them are dressed as fairies. Twice as many people are dressed as cats than are dressed as fairies. If Anna is also dressed as a cat, how many people at the party are dressed as cats? _____

Section 2 Test 4

Target time: 10 minutes

In each group, three words go together and two are the odd ones out. Underline the **two** words that do **not** go with the other three.

Example scalding, sweltering, <u>bitter</u>, <u>raw</u>, roasting

1. scarlet, indigo, crimson, mauve, violet
2. friend, employee, neighbour, colleague, worker
3. present, gift, future, ornament, past
4. hive, nest, ground, burrow, sky
5. discuss, disgust, repulse, repel, replace

Underline the pair of words that are most **similar** in meaning.

Example (sent, puncture)   (fascinate, fasten)   (<u>perfume</u>, <u>scent</u>)

6. (exchange, accept)   (grant, panic)   (buy, purchase)
7. (invaluable, priceless)   (bargain, prize)   (payment, expense)
8. (chimney, factory)   (buzz, electric)   (industrious, busy)
9. (space, patient)   (gate, hotel)   (residence, dwelling)
10. (mouldy, moss)   (rot, decay)   (dusty, declare)

Underline the two words, **one** from each group, that will complete the sentence in the best way.

Example **Detective** is to (inspector, crime, <u>investigate</u>) as **tutor** is to (acrobatics, <u>teach</u>, expect).

11. **London** is to (global, England, Parliament) as **Paris** is to (France, Europe, fashion).
12. **Spoon** is to (stir, prepare, chef) as **spade** is to (cards, gardener, hole).
13. **Africa** is to (continent, sea, lioness) as **New York** is to (America, city, town).
14. **Mountain** is to (steep, horizon, mountaineer) as **sea** is to (navigate, sailor, reef).

Some letters are missing from the words below. Use the word's definition to help you fill in the missing letters. Write the word on the line.

Example G __ __ E __ __ US   giving, charitable   _____GENEROUS_____

15. F __ R __ U __ __ T __ L __   luckily, thankfully, providentially   _____
16. E __ LIG __ T __ __ __ D   open-minded, tolerant   _____

Section 2 Test 5

Target time: 10 minutes

Work out the missing number and write it on the line.

Example 36 [6] 6   45 [9] 5   25 [__5__] 5
($a \div b = ?$, where a represents the number on the left and b represents the number on the right)

1. 24 [6] 4   90 [3] 30   15 [_____] 5
2. 7 [28] 4   8 [48] 6   7 [_____] 8
3. 56 [6] 50   25 [5] 20   85 [_____] 80
4. 77 [11] 7   18 [9] 2   21 [_____] 3
5. 175 [180] 5   190 [199] 9   84 [_____] 66

Rearrange the word in capitals to make another word that goes with the first two. Write the new word on the line.

Example bulb   light   PALM   __LAMP__

6. thyme   rosemary   AGES   _____
7. harvest   sow   PEAR   _____
8. bike   horse   DIRE   _____
9. dogs   pets   ACTS   _____
10. look   see   RATES   _____

Underline the words in brackets that will complete the sentence in the best way.

Example The (<u>baby</u>, man, elephant) was asleep in his (bath, <u>cot</u>, tree).

11. The (mouse, horse, cat) galloped through the (road, grass, stable).
12. The boy kicked the (ball, orange, foot) into the (table, grass, net).
13. Gran went to the (library, shop, post office) to post the (cheese, letter, cat).
14. Mum put the (milk, cake, butter) into the (oven, fridge, bath) to bake.

Work out the answers. Write your answers on the lines.

15. Four girls are competing in a race. Jane is winning. Jane is 2 seconds ahead of Sasha, who is 1 second behind Lola. Edith is 3 seconds behind Sasha. Who is in second place? _____

16. Four children line up in height order from shortest to tallest. Sophie is the shortest of the group. Fred is shorter than Callum but taller than Grace. Who stands at the back of the line? _____

Score: Time taken: Target met?

Verbal Reasoning Rapid Tests 4 Answers

Notes for parents, tutors, teachers and other adult helpers

- **Verbal Reasoning Rapid Tests 4** is designed for nine- and ten-year-olds, but may also be suitable for some older children.
- Remove this pull-out section before giving the book to the child.
- Before the child begins work on the first test, read together the instructions on page 2, headed **What to do**. As you do so, look together at **Section 1 Test 1** and point out to the child the different elements.
- As each question type is introduced for the first time within a particular test, an example is given. Where question types recur throughout the book, the same example is provided. This is deliberate: the example will act as a useful reminder, but children will not need to work through it repeatedly from scratch.
- Make sure that the child understands how to answer the questions and that he or she has a pencil, an eraser and a sheet of rough paper. You should also ensure that the child is able to see a clock or a watch.
- Explain to the child how he or she should go about timing the test. Alternatively, you may wish to time the test yourself. When the child has finished the test, you should together work out the **Time taken** and complete the box that appears at the end of the test.
- Mark the child's work using this pull-out section, giving one mark for each correct answer unless instructed otherwise. There are a total of 16 marks available for each test. Then complete the **Score** box at the end of the test.
- The table below shows you how to mark the **Target met?** box and the **Action** notes help you to plan the next step. However, these are suggestions only. Please use your own judgement as you decide how best to proceed.

Score	Time taken	Target met?	Action
1–8	Any	Not yet	Give the child the previous book in the series. Provide help and support as needed.
9–13	Any	Not yet	Encourage the child to keep practising using the tests in this book. The child may need to repeat some tests. If so, wait a few weeks, or the child may simply remember the correct answers. Provide help and support as needed.
14–16	Over target – child took too long	Not yet	
14–16	On target – child took suggested time or less	Yes	Encourage the child to keep practising using further tests in this book, and to move on to the next book when you think this is appropriate.

- After finishing each test, the child should fill in the **Progress chart** on page 40.
- Whatever the test score, always encourage the child to have another go at the questions that he or she got wrong – without looking at the solutions. If the child's answers are still incorrect, work through these questions together. Demonstrate the correct method if necessary.
- If the child struggles with particular question types, help him or her to develop the strategies needed.

Answers

Section 1 Test 1
(page 4)
1. depart, leave
2. accelerate, quicken
3. enrage, anger
4. ancient, old
5. brave, courageous
6. BAR (BARN)
7. RUN (RUNNING)
8. LET (LETTER)
9. LIP (SLIPPERY)
10. HAT (THAT)
11. −5 (−15)
12. 243 (×3)
13. 25 (repeating pattern +3, +4)
14. 2.5 (+0.5 each time)
15. 5
16. blue, green and yellow

Section 1 Test 2
(page 5)
1. 2
2. 3
3. 3
4. 1
5. 2
6. exit, enter
7. super, awful
8. sell, buy
9. tiny, gigantic
10. hero, villain
11. 1533
12. 4357
13. 8953
14. FLAW
15. D
16. D

Section 1 Test 3
(page 6)
1. instrument, tool
2. pin, tar
3. write, knight (homophones)
4. green, red
5. scales, fur
6. B (10 + 3 = 13)
7. B (24 ÷ 2 = 12)
8. C (100 ÷ 2 = 50)
9. E (80 × 2 = 160)
10. D (99 ÷ 9 = 11)
11. FB (two patterns leapfrog +1, same; +1, same)
12. XP (two patterns leapfrog +1, +1; +1, +1)
13. EN (+1, −3)
14. JH (+2, −2)
15. 4.05 p.m./five past four/16:05
16. 35 seconds

Section 1 Test 4
(page 7)
1. heavy, light
2. answer, question
3. slow, rapid
4. sweet, bitter
5. certain, doubtful
6. n
7. d
8. m
9. e
10. f
11. RE (−4, −4)
12. HR (+3, +3)
13. HT (−5, −5)
14. XS (+2, +3)
15. 121
16. 5

Section 1 Test 5
(page 8)
1. wish (How is his dog?)
2. star (Her train was the last arrival.)
3. pout (Parachutists jump out of planes.)
4. lean (My uncle answered the phone.)
5. hone (Which one is yours?)
6. pore, rope
7. pale, leap
8. lope, pole
9. mile, lime
10. save, vase

11. 81 (a × b)
12. 11 (a ÷ b)
13. 1 (a ÷ b)
14. 45 (a − b)
15. 11
16. Friday

Section 1 Test 6
(page 9)
1. AIR (PAIR)
2. BEE (BEEN)
3. BEG (BEGINS)
4. FIR (FIRE)
5. ATE (WATER)
6. viewpoint
7. necklace
8. paperclip
9. fairground
10. helpline
11. 10
12. 5
13. 3
14. 4
15. B
16. A

Section 1 Test 7
(page 10)
1. train
2. tick
3. scrabble
4. read
5. head
6. always, never (the other words are all prepositions)
7. ferret, hamster (the others are all birds)
8. office, barn (the others are all types of homes)
9. quiver, chain (the others are all instruments)
10. rectangle, circle (the others are all 3D shapes)
11. sign
12. coin
13. grin
14. wink
15. 2
16. 38

Answers

Section 1 Test 8 (page 11)
1. shake, quiver
2. embrace, hug
3. peak, summit
4. real, genuine
5. livid, furious
6. GLUE [BLUE] BLUB
7. WINK [PINK] PUNK
8. BOAT [MOAT] MOST
9. WILD [MILD] MILK
10. LOVE [LONE] LONG
11. OVW (mirror code)
12. VZG (mirror code)
13. SRG (mirror code)
14. NZM (mirror code)
15. 9 p.m./nine o'clock/21:00
16. 25 minutes

Section 1 Test 9 (page 12)
1. vanilla
2. wheeze
3. revolting
4. murmur
5. scrape
6. 10
7. 3
8. 2
9. 1
10. 8
11. PM (two patterns leapfrog +1, +1; −1, +1)
12. QJ (+1, +1)
13. CM (two patterns leapfrog −1, −1; +1, +1)
14. MH (+2, +2)
15. 2
16. 4

Section 1 Test 10 (page 13)
1. pliers, spanner (the others are kitchen utensils)
2. banner, flag (the others are tools)
3. decrease, reduce (the others all refer to making something higher)
4. frozen, cold (the other words describe heat)
5. miserable, sad (the other words describe cheerful feelings)
6. AIL (SAILOR)
7. AGE (MARRIAGE)
8. ANT (IMPORTANT)
9. ONE (LONELY)
10. WAS (WASTE)
11. NWJ (+1, +2, +3, etc. from the word to the code)
12. WTUJ (+5 from the word to the code)
13. SAME (repeating pattern of +1, +2, +1, +2 from the code to the word)
14. VFHRD (repeating pattern of −1, −2, −1, −2 from the word to the code)
15. ASTONISHED
16. INTELLIGENT

Section 1 Test 11 (page 14)
1. ram, cold (move c)
2. river, dripping (move d)
3. bead, drone (move r)
4. bid, through (move r)
5. low, bang (move g)
6. D (10 + 4 ÷ 2 = 7)
7. B (20 + 2 ÷ 11 = 2)
8. A (50 − 5 ÷ 5 = 9)
9. E (172 − 2 ÷ 10 = 17)
10. E (9 + 11 + 12 = 32)
11. mice
12. fist
13. raid
14. flog
15. 4
16. 2

Section 1 Test 12 (page 15)
1. failure
2. fresh
3. spend
4. remember
5. innocent
6. n
7. c
8. t
9. d
10. w
11. YLZG (mirror code)
12. XSZRI (mirror code)
13. NZIP (mirror code)
14. LETTER (mirror code)
15. Amelia
16. Lewis

Section 2 Test 1 (page 16)
1. 72 (repeated pattern ×2, ×3)
2. 72 (two patterns leapfrog ×2)
3. 40 (−12)
4. 4000 (÷2)
5. 9.25 (+0.25)
6. solid
7. heart
8. island
9. fireplace
10. netball
11. 3251
12. 3128
13. 4155
14. SLEEP
15. C
16. A

Verbal Reasoning Rapid Tests 4 Answers

Answers

Section 2 Test 2 (page 17)

1. alter
2. melody
3. cease
4. talent
5. capable
6. horns, antlers
7. scorching, freezing
8. rubber, glass
9. hospital, school
10. aunt, father
11. OZ (two patterns leapfrog +1, same; +1, +1)
12. ZR (+1, +8/−8)
13. QC (+1, −4)
14. UB (two patterns leapfrog +1, +1)
15. 22 days
16. 20 September

Section 2 Test 3 (page 18)

1–5. [score half a point for each correct answer]
A = ball game
B = winter sport
C = water sport
skiing = B,
windsurfing = C,
football = A,
snowboarding = B,
swimming = C,
snorkelling = C,
netball = A,
tobogganing = B,
rugby = A, rafting = C
6. E (12 ÷ 2 × 0 = 0)
7. D (10 ÷ 2 × 5 = 25)
8. E (8 × 2 × 2 = 32)
9. D (12 − 2 × 10 = 100)
10. E (5 × 9 × 10 = 450)
11. GS (−3, −2)
12. WY (mirror code)
13. TI (−4, −2)
14. IT (+5, +3)
15. 5
16. 11

Section 2 Test 4 (page 19)

1. scarlet, crimson (the other words refer to shades of purple)
2. friend, neighbour (the others are all people in the workplace)
3. gift, ornament (the other words are to do with time)
4. ground, sky (the others are animals' homes)
5. discuss, replace (the other words describe feelings of dislike)
6. buy, purchase
7. invaluable, priceless
8. industrious, busy
9. residence, dwelling
10. rot, decay
11. England, France
12. chef, gardener
13. continent, city
14. mountaineer, sailor
15. FORTUNATELY
16. ENLIGHTENED

Section 2 Test 5 (page 20)

1. 3 (a ÷ b)
2. 56 (a × b)
3. 5 (a − b)
4. 7 (a ÷ b)
5. 150 (a + b)
6. SAGE
7. REAP
8. RIDE
9. CATS
10. STARE
11. horse, grass
12. ball, net
13. post office, letter
14. cake, oven
15. Lola
16. Callum

Section 2 Test 6 (page 21)

1. WISH [FISH] FIST
2. LOOP [HOOP] HOOD
3. GAIN [RAIN] REIN
4. DUST [MUST] MUSE
5. MARK [DARK] DARN
6. lipstick
7. wristwatch
8. shoelace
9. heathen
10. automobile
11. lifeguard
12. brother
13. science
14. twig
15. 3
16. 9

Section 2 Test 7 (page 22)

1. nice (When ice melts it turns back into liquid.)
2. wife (Do you know if everyone has gone?)
3. mess (When water freezes it becomes solid.)
4. wasp (I was pretending not to hear the doorbell.)
5. beak (Ben wished he could be a knight.)
6. bean, king (move g)
7. tan, thin (move h)
8. room, black (move b)
9. sea, melt (move l)
10. are, sheep (move h)
11. r
12. w
13. p
14. k
15. 10
16. 26

Answers

Section 2 Test 8 (page 23)
1. past
2. accept
3. vanish
4. loose
5. grief
6. CUT (ACUTE)
7. ATE (AFFECTIONATE)
8. WON (WONDER)
9. RED (FIRED)
10. ARM (ARMOUR)
11. swam, ocean
12. tractor, field, barn
13. magician, appear, hat
14. zoo, animals
15. 11.15 a.m./quarter past eleven/11:15
16. 3 hours 30 minutes/3 and a half hours

Section 2 Test 9 (page 24)
1. are, cage (move c)
2. all, year (move y)
3. fail, drown (move r)
4. bath, crow (move c)
5. muse, droop (move o)
6. weakness, character (the others refer to abilities)
7. paint, mirror (the others are all types of pictures)
8. guilty, excited (the others are all words to do with worry)
9. floor, precise (the others are all to do with negative things)
10. bland, tasteless (the others describe tasty food)
11. 17 (repeating pattern +6, −3)
12. 127 (×2 and +1 each time)
13. 110 (−11)
14. 44 (+6)
15. B
16. D

Section 2 Test 10 (page 25)
1. cold (A magic old man is a wizard.)
2. mask (The groom asked for some wedding cake.)
3. drag (He found ragged clothes in the dustbin.)
4. rang (That corner has a wider angle.)
5. late (I can feel a tender spot there.)
6. summertime
7. horseshoe
8. bathtub
9. gentlemen
10. earring
11. August, March
12. lungs, gills
13. think, chew
14. amid, able (anagrams)
15. 6
16. 27 May

Section 2 Test 11 (page 26)
1. JE (−1, +1)
2. QS (+1, +2)
3. DN (two patterns leapfrog −1, −1; −1, −1)
4. NH (two patterns leapfrog +2, +2; +1, +2)
5. QN (two patterns leapfrog +1, +1; −1, +1)
6. 8
7. 3
8. 12
9. 5
10. 2
11. earl
12. draw
13. tuck
14. duel
15. 18 days
16. 15

Section 2 Test 12 (page 27)
1. RS (mirror code)
2. RN (−3, +3)
3. YV (+2, −2)
4. OQ (mirror code)
5. PX (mirror code)
6. the pleased (I am pleased you passed the test!)
7. gracefully butterflies (The butterflies fluttered by gracefully.)
8. Polly dog (My dog is called Polly.)
9. leave train (When will the train to London leave?)
10. tail cat (My pet cat has no tail.)
11. battle
12. fortunate
13. material
14. whip
15. 22
16. Lucy and Sam (at 11.05 a.m.)

Section 3 Test 1 (page 28)
1–5. [score half a point for each correct answer]
A = keyboard
B = string
C = wind
organ = A, mandolin = B, banjo = B, guitar = B, saxophone = C, clarinet = C, cello = B, trombone = C, accordion = A, tuba = C
6. trip (Can you see that ripple in the water?)
7. test (My brother creates too much mess.)
8. here (I gave her a handkerchief to dab her eyes.)
9. rake (I can hear a kestrel's call.)
10. dart (She painted artistic images.)

Verbal Reasoning Rapid Tests 4 Answers

Answers

11. BEOL (repeating pattern of +3, +0 from the word to the code)
12. WAND (repeating pattern of −3, −0 from the code to the word)
13. KFXHP (decreasing gaps +6, +5, +4, +3, +2 from the word to the code)
14. YEPA (decreasing gaps −5, −4, −3, −2 from the word to the code)
15. Sylvie
16. James

Section 3 Test 2 (page 29)

1. 160 (a − b)
2. 2 (a ÷ b)
3. 183 (a − b)
4. 99 (a × b)
5. 144 (a × b)
6. CRIME
7. RACE
8. LAKE
9. CARDS
10. SOAP
11. ART (APART)
12. OAR (COARSE)
13. CON (CONVERSATION)
14. FOR (FORCED)
15. 2 hours and 40 minutes
16. 18

Section 3 Test 3 (page 30)

1. sand, trail (move t)
2. ride, table (move b)
3. oak, flaps (move s)
4. chose, orange (move o)
5. apple, changed (move d)
6. s
7. t
8. m
9. h
10. g
11. 3964
12. 5149
13. 3649

14. PLEAT
15. ACCIDENTAL
16. INTERLOPER

Section 3 Test 4 (page 31)

1. lock
2. cracker
3. music
4. brown
5. sky
6. JP (+4, −4)
7. TZ (−2, +3)
8. YP (mirror code)
9. PK (+1, −2)
10. ZU (mirror code)
11. for
12. up
13. end
14. out
15. 14
16. 10

Section 3 Test 5 (page 32)

1. very film (The film had a very sad ending.)
2. called best (My best friend is called Megan.)
3. eat spin (Spiders spin their webs and eat flies.)
4. smells perfume (Your new perfume smells lovely.)
5. eggs chicken (The chicken laid four eggs.)
6. D (35 ÷ 5 × 2 = 14)
7. D (12 × 12 − 12 = 132)
8. B (77 ÷ 11 + 9 = 16)
9. A (1 × 32 × 0 = 0)
10. C (40 ÷ 2 + 4 = 24)
11. LQ (two patterns leapfrog −1, −1; +2, +2)
12. QP (two patterns leapfrog +2, +2; +2, +2)
13. WU (−1, −1)
14. DE (+3, +1)
15. Mitch
16. Mae

Section 3 Test 6 (page 33)

1. keen, eager
2. wail, howl
3. alarm, worry
4. danger, hazard
5. affection, fondness
6. Pluto
7. Paris
8. jewel
9. ruby
10. twenty
11. GLASSES (repeating pattern of −2, −0 from the code to the word)
12. DJHIPY (increasing gaps +1, +2, +3, etc. from the word to the code)
13. TIGHTS (repeating pattern of −1, −0 from the code to the word)
14. BHQBTR (−1 from the word to the code)
15. 21
16. 11 September

Section 3 Test 7 (page 34)

1. over
2. post
3. con
4. can
5. bar
6. e
7. y
8. n
9. r
10. d
11. heat (The athlete was very fit.)
12. dead (The businessmen made a deal.)
13. bean (Why do you want to be a nurse?)
14. kiss (Jack is sensible enough to walk to school by himself.)
15. 1 hour and 40 minutes/100 minutes

A6 Schofield & Sims

Answers

16. 8.15 p.m./quarter past eight/20:15

Section 3 Test 8 (page 35)

1. 50 (a ÷ b)
2. 14 (a + 2b)
3. 13 (2a + b)
4. 12 (a + b + 1)
5. 15 (a − b − 1)
6. home, abroad
7. adore, hate
8. sharp, blunt
9. friend, foe
10. famous, unknown
11. REAR [FEAR] FEAT
12. SINK [SUNK] BUNK
13. RING [RANG] GANG
14. KIND [WIND] WINE
15. 3 socks (one of the pairs plus the odd sock)
16. 2

Section 3 Test 9 (page 36)

1. racket
2. direction
3. custom
4. arrangement
5. concern
6. den, sett
7. stream, pond
8. been, seem (homophones)
9. drove, slept
10. dig, hammer
11. lone
12. gown
13. rate
14. rind
15. April
16. 24 July

Section 3 Test 10 (page 37)

1. C (40 ÷ 2 + 4 = 24)
2. D (100 − 25 − 5 = 70)
3. A (88 ÷ 11 + 3 = 11)
4. C (3 + 23 − 26 = 0)
5. A (64 ÷ 2 + 12 = 44)

6. balance, incline (the others describe thin objects)
7. fare, bill (the others are all about equality)
8. bland, brash (the others describe a happy state)
9. fish, capture (the others are all to do with climbing up)
10. outrage, shock (the others are about shouting)
11. FU (+3, −1)
12. SA (−4, +3)
13. MY (+5, −2)
14. FK (mirror code)
15. 36 tiles (5.5 × 6.5 = 35.75m² which rounds up to 36 tiles)
16. £10 (original price was £40: 25% of £40 = £10; £40 − £10 = £30)

Section 3 Test 11 (page 38)

1. trap, swam
2. ate, for (homophones)
3. sight, hearing
4. assist, harm
5. flies, grass
6. 56 (+7)
7. 800 (×2)
8. 6 (two patterns leapfrog ÷2, ÷3)
9. 22 (repeating pattern of −3, ×2)
10. 7 (repeating pattern of ÷2, −4)
11. f
12. e
13. p
14. h
15. 29
16. 6

Section 3 Test 12 (page 39)

1. 1
2. 8
3. 2
4. 8
5. 1
6. continue, cease
7. reveal, hide
8. seldom, often
9. permanent, temporary
10. open, secretive
11. 56741
12. 58648
13. 41867
14. PEACH
15–16. A and B

Verbal Reasoning Rapid Tests 4 Answers

This book of answers is a pull-out section from
Verbal Reasoning Rapid Tests 4

Published by **Schofield & Sims Ltd**,
7 Mariner Court, Wakefield, West Yorkshire WF4 3FL, UK
Telephone 01484 607080
www.schofieldandsims.co.uk

First published in 2014
This edition copyright © Schofield & Sims Ltd, 2018
Seventh impression 2023

Author: **Siân Goodspeed.** *Siân Goodspeed has asserted her moral right under the Copyright, Designs and Patents Act, 1988, to be identified as the author of this work.*

British Library Cataloguing in Publication Data. *A catalogue record for this book is available from the British Library.*

All rights reserved. No part of this publication may be reproduced, stored in a retrieval system, or transmitted in any form or by any means, electronic, mechanical, photocopying, recording or otherwise, without either the prior permission of the publisher or a licence permitting restricted copying in the United Kingdom issued by the Copyright Licensing Agency Ltd.

Commissioned by **Carolyn Richardson Publishing Services**
Design by **Oxford Designers & Illustrators**
Printed in the UK by **Page Bros (Norwich) Ltd**
ISBN 978 07217 1453 0

Section 2 Test 6

Target time: 10 minutes

Change the first word into the last word by changing only **one** letter at a time, making a new word in the middle. Write the new word on the line.

Example LAKE [__LANE__] PANE

1. WISH [_____] FIST
2. LOOP [_____] HOOD
3. GAIN [_____] REIN
4. DUST [_____] MUSE
5. MARK [_____] DARN

Underline the two words, **one** from each group, that together make one new word. The word from the first group comes first.

Example (<u>kit</u>, pip, nine)   (comic, <u>ten</u>, numb)   (kitten)

6. (lip, tongue, cheek)   (branch, leaf, stick)
7. (wrist, arm, hand)   (look, see, watch)
8. (foot, sole, shoe)   (dress, lace, bride)
9. (hot, warm, heat)   (hen, sun, food)
10. (mechanic, auto, done)   (mobile, move, phone)

If these words were listed in alphabetical order, which word would come **last**? Write the answer on the line.

Example kite   colourful   breeze   blow   chase   __kite__

11. dentist   doctor   lawyer   farmer   lifeguard   _____
12. born   birthday   baby   brother   bottle   _____
13. English   history   science   geography   school   _____
14. tree   leaf   life   twig   plant   _____

Work out the answers. Write your answers on the lines.

15. A bride has a bouquet of 12 flowers. Half the flowers are roses. 3 are petunias. The rest are tulips. How many flowers are tulips? _____
16. When Maria is 9, her sister will be 13. Her mother is 33 and her cousin is 15. How old will Maria's twin brother be, when her sister is 13? _____

Score: Time taken: Target met?

Verbal Reasoning Rapid Tests 4

Section 2 Test 7

Target time: 10 minutes

Find the **four-letter word** hidden across two or more consecutive words in each sentence below. The order of the letters must stay the same. Underline the word and write it on the line.

Example You certainly <u>do lead</u> an interesting life.   _dole_

1. When ice melts it turns back into liquid. _____
2. Do you know if everyone has gone? _____
3. When water freezes it becomes solid. _____
4. I was pretending not to hear the doorbell. _____
5. Ben wished he could be a knight. _____

Move one letter from the first word to the second word to make two new words. Do not reorder the letters. Write the two new words on the lines.

Example spray, eat   _pray_ , _seat_   (move the s)

6. began, kin   _____ , _____
7. than, tin   _____ , _____
8. broom, lack   _____ , _____
9. seal, met   _____ , _____
10. hare, seep   _____ , _____

Find **one** missing letter that completes **both** pairs of words. Write it on the lines.

Example tre [_e_] asy   lik [_e_] ver   (tree and easy, like and ever)

11. gea [__] ocket   stee [__] iver   13. sni [__] lunge   troo [__] ress
12. shado [__] age   kne [__] ither   14. pin [__] ept   attac [__] nit

Work out the answers. Write your answers on the lines.

15. Jenna, Joel and Pedro all collect stickers. Jenna has 17 flower stickers and 8 car stickers. Joel has 15 car stickers. Pedro has half as many stickers as Jenna and Joel have together. Half of Pedro's stickers are animal stickers. How many animal stickers does Pedro have? _____

16. Benny is a mechanic. Today he has fixed 3 green cars and 2 motorbikes. Yesterday he fixed 2 red cars and a motorbike. None of the vehicles he fixed were missing any wheels. How many wheels did the vehicles that Benny fixed have altogether? _____

Score: Time taken: Target met?

Section 2 Test 8

Target time: 10 minutes

Underline the word in brackets that is most **opposite** in meaning to the word in capitals.

Example AGITATED (tiger, calm, vague, eager, peace)

1. FUTURE (tomorrow, week, later, month, past)
2. REFUSE (reflect, accept, believe, declare, report)
3. APPEAR (vain, vanish, sincere, hidden, disguise)
4. TIGHT (lose, curved, sock, loose, clingy)
5. JOY (celebration, like, grief, jealousy, guilty)

In each of the sentences below, the word in capitals has three letters missing. Those three letters spell a word. Write the three-letter word on the line.

Example Sally **M D** the lawn.   ___OWE___   (MOWED)

6. The triangle had an **A E** angle. _____
7. Her pet dog was **AFFECTION**. _____
8. I **D E R** what time we are leaving? _____
9. The lazy worker was **F I**. _____
10. The arrow pierced the soldier's **O U R**. _____

Underline the words in brackets that will complete the sentence in the best way.

Example The (baby, man, elephant) was asleep in his (bath, cot, tree).

11. The dolphin (jumped, swam, walked) gracefully through the (ocean, pond, puddle).
12. The farmer drove the (bicycle, tractor, boat) across the (lake, garden, field) to the (shop, barn, beach).
13. The (teacher, nurse, magician) made a rabbit (vanishing, appear, furry) out of his (hat, beard, playground).
14. The class went to the (shop, pool, zoo) to see the (queen, doctor, animals).

Work out the answers. Write your answers on the lines.

15. It is 14:15 now. What time was it 3 hours ago? _____
16. It takes Jazib 1 hour and 10 minutes to paint 1 wall in his square bedroom. If he works at the same pace throughout, how long will it take him to paint the other 3 walls? _____

Score: Time taken: Target met?

Verbal Reasoning Rapid Tests 4   23

Section 2 Test 9

Target time: 10 minutes

Move one letter from the first word to the second word to make two new words. Do not reorder the letters. Write the two new words on the lines.

Example spray, eat ____pray____ , ____seat____ (move the s)

1. care, age   _____ , _____   4. batch, row   _____ , _____
2. ally, ear   _____ , _____   5. mouse, drop   _____ , _____
3. frail, down   _____ , _____

In each group, three words go together and two are the odd ones out. Underline the **two** words that do **not** go with the other three.

Example scalding, sweltering, <u>bitter</u>, <u>raw</u>, roasting

6. talent, ability, weakness, skill, character
7. sketch, portrait, paint, image, mirror
8. nervous, guilty, anxious, alarmed, excited
9. blemish, floor, flaw, precise, fault
10. bland, appetising, delicious, scrumptious, tasteless

Find the missing number in the sequence. Write it on the line.

Example 32   28   20   16   8   __4__   (repeating pattern −4, −8)

11. 5   11   8   14   11   ____   14   20
12. 7   15   31   63   ____   255
13. 132 121 ____ 99   88   77
14. 14   20   26   32   38   ____

Circle the letter next to the **true** statement for each question.

15. All reptiles lay eggs. A snake is a type of reptile.

    If the above statements are true, which one of the following statements must also be true?
    A Baby snakes eat eggs.   C Snakes like swimming.
    B Snakes lay eggs.   D Snake eggs are blue.

16. Plants and animals that live in water are aquatic. Coral is an animal that lives in water.

    If the above statements are true, which one of the following statements must also be true?
    A Coral is a kind of flower.   C Coral comes in many colours.
    B Fish live in aquariums.   D Coral is aquatic.

Score: _____   Time taken: _____   Target met? _____

Section 2 Test 10

Target time: 10 minutes

Find the **four-letter word** hidden across two or more consecutive words in each sentence below. The order of the letters must stay the same. Underline the word and write it on the line.

Example You certainly <u>do l</u>ead an interesting life.   ____dole____

1. A magic old man is a wizard. _____
2. The groom asked for some wedding cake. _____
3. He found ragged clothes in the dustbin. _____
4. That corner has a wider angle. _____
5. I can feel a tender spot there. _____

Underline the two words, **one** from each group, that together make one new word. The word from the first group comes first.

Example (<u>kit</u>, pip, nine)   (comic, <u>ten</u>, numb)   (kitten)

6. (summer, sun, light)   (shone, time, month)
7. (pony, horse, farm)   (foot, show, shoe)
8. (bath, sink, tap)   (box, tub, pot)
9. (gentle, soft, nice)   (house, coach, men)
10. (ear, face, hear)   (wring, ring, sing)

Underline the two words, **one** from each group, that will complete the sentence in the best way.

Example **Detective** is to (inspector, crime, <u>investigate</u>) as **tutor** is to (acrobatics, <u>teach</u>, expect).

11. **July** is to (festival, August, June) as **February** is to (April, romantic, March).
12. **Mammal** is to (purr, lungs, pet) as **fish** is to (chips, gills, salt).
13. **Brain** is to (skull, massive, think) as **teeth** are to (chew, dentist, pointy).
14. **Maid** is to (mix, amid, dust) as **bale** is to (able, stable, harvest).

Work out the answers. Write your answers on the lines.

15. Leo is twice Carl's age. If Leo is 12, how old is Carl? _____
16. Luke's kitten, Flash, is 3 weeks old today. If Flash was born on 6 May, what is the date today? _____

Score: Time taken: Target met?

Verbal Reasoning Rapid Tests 4

Section 2 Test 11

Target time: 10 minutes

Find the missing letter pair in the sequence. Write it on the line. Use the alphabet to help you.

A B C D E F G H I J K L M N O P Q R S T U V W X Y Z

Example JP   ML   PH   SD   VZ   __YV__   (+3, −4)

1. LC   KD   _____   IF   HG   GH
2. OO   PQ   _____   RU   SW   TY
3. FP   ZZ   EO   AA   _____   BB   CM
4. HB   JF   JD   KH   LF   LJ   _____
5. NK   ZY   OL   YZ   PM   XA   _____

Find the missing number in each equation. Write the number on the line.

Example 72 + 3 = 25 × __3__   (72 + 3 = 75 and so does 25 × 3)

6. 88 ÷ 8 = 19 − _____
7. 18 ÷ 9 = 6 ÷ _____
8. 27 ÷ 9 = 15 − _____
9. 70 ÷ 10 = 2 + _____
10. 17 + 2 + 1 = 40 ÷ _____

Make a new word by changing the first word of the third pair in the same way as the other pairs. Write the new word on the line.

Example wider, weir   waver, wear   fault, __flat__   (take the 1st, 4th, 2nd, 5th letters)

11. editor, diet   spates, past   really, _____
12. rails, liar   garble, brag   warden, _____
13. shrugs, hugs   scrape, cape   struck, _____
14. dread, dear   treat, tear   clued, _____

Work out the answers. Write your answers on the lines.

15. Martin is looking forward to his party on 18 December. If it is 30 November today, how long is it until his party? _____
16. Jon is 5 years older than Leanne, who is 1 year older than Simon. If Simon is 9, how old is Jon? _____

Score: Time taken: Target met?

26   Schofield & Sims

Section 2 Test 12

Target time: 10 minutes

Using the alphabet to help you, find the letters that complete each sentence. Write the letters on the line. You might need to use a different method from the example given.

A B C D E F G H I J K L M N O P Q R S T U V W X Y Z

Example JB is to PY as KR is to __QO__.   (+6, −3)

1. AG is to ZT as IH is to _____.
2. NN is to KQ as UK is to _____.
3. LM is to NK as WX is to _____.
4. FB is to UY as LJ is to _____.
5. MG is to NT as KC is to _____.

Underline the **two** words in each sentence that need to change places in order for the sentence to make sense.

Example How <u>ticket</u> is a train <u>much</u> to London?   (How much is a train ticket to London?)

6. I am the you passed pleased test!
7. The gracefully fluttered by butterflies.
8. My Polly is called dog.
9. When will the leave to London train?
10. My pet tail has no cat.

Underline the word in brackets that is **closest** in meaning to the word in capitals.

Example SCENT   (puncture, <u>perfume</u>, sent, fascinate)

11. COMBAT   (ambush, figure, army, battle, victory)
12. LUCKY   (clover, fortunate, plain, glamorous, buttercup)
13. FABRIC   (needle, thread, material, evidence, invent)
14. LASH   (whip, crack, lightning, eye, shove)

Work out the answers. Write your answers on the lines.

15. Marie's exam was in the hall, with Jacob and Stephanie. Andrew and his 17 classmates had a science exam in the lab. Waahida was also in the lab with 3 of her friends. How many people were in the lab? _____

16. Lucy leaves the house at 9.55 a.m. and gets to school one hour and 10 minutes later. Kristoff gets to school at 10 a.m. after a 20-minute journey from home. Sam leaves the house at 10.20 a.m. and has a 45-minute journey. Which two students arrive at school at the same time? _____ and _____

Score: ____   Time taken: ____   Target met? ____

Verbal Reasoning Rapid Tests 4

Section 3 Test 1

Target time: 10 minutes

1–5. Look at the words in groups A, B and C. For each of the words below, choose the correct group and write its letter on the line.

A	B	C
piano	violin	trumpet

organ _____   mandolin _____   banjo _____   guitar _____   saxophone _____
clarinet _____   cello _____   trombone _____   accordion _____   tuba _____

Find the **four-letter word** hidden across two or more consecutive words in each sentence below. The order of the letters must stay the same. Underline the word and write it on the line.

Example You certainly <u>do le</u>ad an interesting life.   _____dole_____

6. Can you see that ripple in the water?   _____
7. My brother creates too much mess.   _____
8. I gave her a handkerchief to dab her eyes.   _____
9. I can hear a kestrel's call.   _____
10. She painted artistic images.   _____

Using the alphabet to help you, crack the code. You might need to use a different method from the example given. Write your answer on the line.

A B C D E F G H I J K L M N O P Q R S T U V W X Y Z

Example If the code for **CART** is **EZTS**, what is the code for **KING**?   __MHPF__ (+2, −1, +2, −1)

11. If the code for **SCREAM** is **VCUEDM**, what is the code for **YELL**? _____
12. If the code **PAJIF** means **MAGIC**, what does the code **ZAQD** mean? _____
13. If **DRINK** is written in code as **JWMQM**, what is the code for **EATEN**? _____
14. If the code for **BAND** is **WWKB**, what is the code for **DISC**? _____

Work out the answers. Write your answers on the lines.

15. Five children sat an exam at school. Sylvie scored 60 marks. Ali scored better than Sylvie but not as well as Jean. Tanak and Ben both scored less than Sylvie. Who scored the third highest mark in the group? _____

16. Grandpa and his four grandchildren are being served dinner. Grandpa is served his meal first. Charlie gets his meal before Kitty but after James. Kyle is served last. Who is served second? _____

Score: _____   Time taken: _____   Target met? _____

Section 3 Test 2

Target time: 10 minutes

Work out the missing number and write it on the line.

Example 36 [6] 6   45 [9] 5   25 [__5__] 5
(a ÷ b = ?, where a represents the number on the left and b represents the number on the right)

1. 103 [76] 27   197 [143] 54   172 [_____] 12
2. 150 [2] 75   200 [2] 100   50 [_____] 25
3. 200 [82] 118   200 [64] 136   200 [_____] 17
4. 8 [96] 12   9 [81] 9   9 [_____] 11
5. 12 [48] 4   12 [84] 7   12 [_____] 12

Rearrange the letters in capitals to make a new word so that the sentence makes sense. Write the new word on the line.

Example They were running out of **MEIT**.   __TIME__

6. The man was arrested for committing a **MICRE**. _____
7. The **CARE** was more than one hundred laps. _____
8. Swimming is not allowed in the boating **KLAE**. _____
9. Ben received loads of **RADCS** on his birthday. _____
10. The **PASO** stung when it got in Sarah's eyes at bath time. _____

In each of the sentences below, the word in capitals has three letters missing. Those three letters spell a word. Write the three-letter word on the line.

Example Sally **MD** the lawn.   __OWE__   (MOWED)

11. When I picked up the old book it fell **AP**. _____
12. The wood felt rough and **CSE**. _____
13. The **VERSATION** was long and boring. _____
14. The firefighter **CED** the door open. _____

Work out the answers. Write your answers on the lines.

15. It normally takes me 2 hours and 25 minutes to drive to my friend's house. I start the drive in time to arrive at 6.30 p.m. but I am delayed by traffic. If I arrive at 6.45 p.m., how long has the drive taken me today? _____

16. Jesse is typing some emails. It takes him 5 minutes to type one email. How many emails of the same length can he send in an hour and a half? _____

Score: ____   Time taken: ____   Target met? ____

Verbal Reasoning Rapid Tests 4

Section 3 Test 3

Target time: 10 minutes

Move one letter from the first word to the second word to make two new words. Do not reorder the letters. Write the two new words on the lines.

Example spray, eat   ____pray____ , ____seat____   (move the s)

1. stand, rail   _____ , _____
2. bride, tale   _____ , _____
3. soak, flap   _____ , _____
4. choose, range   _____ , _____
5. dapple, change   _____ , _____

Find **one** missing letter that completes **both** pairs of words. Write it on the lines.

Example tre [_e_] asy   lik [_e_] ver   (tree and easy, like and ever)

6. glos [__] peak   spike [__] hort
7. ghos [__] rick   blas [__] remble
8. stor [__] arket   gloo [__] iddle
9. watc [__] over   smas [__] appy
10. flun [__] rave   belon [__] ather

Match the number codes to the words. One code is missing. Use these to work out the answers to the questions. Write your answers on the lines.

SITE   SLIP   TELL   LATE   4639   7139   7415

11–13. What is the code for: **TEAL**? _____ **PILE**? _____ **TALE**? _____

14. What does the code **54963** mean? _____

Some letters are missing from the words below. Use the word's definition to help you fill in the missing letters. Write the word on the line.

Example G __ __ E __ __ US   giving, charitable   ____GENEROUS____

15. A __ __ ID __ N __ __ L   unintentional, inadvertent   _____
16. IN __ E __ __ OP __ R   intruder, imposter   _____

Score: _____   Time taken: _____   Target met? _____

Section 3 Test 4

Target time: 10 minutes

If these words were listed in alphabetical order, which word would come **third**? Write the answer on the line.

Example kite   colourful   breeze   blow   chase   _____chase_____

1. key   lock   safe   steal   lead   _____
2. bread   cheese   cream   cracker   ham   _____
3. music   melodic   note   noise   loud   _____
4. pink   brown   blue   black   purple   _____
5. sun   light   sky   star   horizon   _____

Using the alphabet to help you, find the letters that complete each sentence. Write the letters on the line. You might need to use a different method from the example given.

A B C D E F G H I J K L M N O P Q R S T U V W X Y Z

Example JB is to PY as KR is to __QO__.   (+6, −3)

6. OL is to SH as FT is to _____.
7. DH is to BK as VW is to _____.
8. EG is to VT as BK is to _____.
9. ZK is to AI as OM is to _____.
10. DH is to WS as AF is to _____.

Each word below can be changed into a new word by putting another word in **front**. The added word must be the **same** for each word in the row. Find the word and write it on the line.

Example bow   drop   storm   coat   _____rain_____

11. tune   ward   bear   sake   _____
12. on   hill   set   lifting   _____
13. point   less   anger   ear   _____
14. side   let   run   rage   _____

Work out the answers. Write your answers on the lines.

15. David has an older brother called Alex. Alex is three times as old as David's younger sister Molly. David is twice Molly's age. If Alex is 21, how old is David? _____

16. Chayla is baking cupcakes for her birthday party. There will be 98 guests at the party. If Chayla can only bake cupcakes in batches of 10, how many batches of cakes will she have to bake so that every guest can have a cake? _____

Score: Time taken: Target met?

Section 3 Test 5

Target time: 10 minutes

Underline the **two** words in each sentence that need to change places in order for the sentence to make sense.

Example How <u>ticket</u> is a train <u>much</u> to London?   (How much is a train ticket to London?)

1. The very had a film sad ending.
2. My called friend is best Megan.
3. Spiders eat their webs and spin flies.
4. Your new smells perfume lovely.
5. The eggs laid four chicken.

Use the information given to answer the sum. Write your answer as a **letter**.

Example A = 15   B = 29   C = 32   D = 60   E = 8   **D ÷ A × E =** __C__   (60 ÷ 15 × 8 = 32)

6. A = 35   B = 5   C = 7   D = 14   E = 2   **A ÷ B × E =** _____
7. A = 12   B = 144   C = 142   D = 132   E = 134   **A × A − A =** _____
8. A = 9   B = 16   C = 11   D = 17   E = 77   **E ÷ C + A =** _____
9. A = 0   B = 44   C = 45   D = 32   E = 1   **E × D × A =** _____
10. A = 40   B = 2   C = 24   D = 4   E = 26   **A ÷ B + D =** _____

Find the missing letter pair in the sequence. Write it on the line. Use the alphabet to help you.

A B C D E F G H I J K L M N O P Q R S T U V W X Y Z

Example JP   ML   PH   SD   VZ   __YV__   (+3, −4)

11. OT   CD   NS   EF   MR   GH   _____
12. KJ   LP   ML   NR   ON   PT   _____
13. ZX   YW   XV   _____   VT   US
14. XC   AD   _____   GF   JG   MH

Work out the answers. Write your answers on the lines.

15. Lance and his friends are cycling to school. Stuart sets off ahead of the others but is soon overtaken by Lance who is then overtaken by Mitch. Louis overtakes Mitch but then he gets a puncture and has to stop to fix it. Who gets to school first? _____

16. Saia and her friends are climbing up the monkey bars in the school gym. Laya is two rungs above Mae who is on the rung below Saia. Saia is two rungs below Shelly who is three rungs behind Mica. Who is on the lowest rung? _____

Score: _____   **Time taken:** _____   **Target met?** _____

Section 3 Test 6

Target time: 10 minutes

Underline the pair of words that are most **similar** in meaning.

Example (sent, puncture)   (fascinate, fasten)   (<u>perfume, scent</u>)

1. (sharp, dull)   (keen, eager)   (clean, varnish)
2. (wail, howl)   (shovel, grouch)   (whale, seal)
3. (arm, limp)   (weapon, fire)   (alarm, worry)
4. (slept, awaken)   (danger, hazard)   (dizzy, twisted)
5. (affection, fondness)   (careful, adoption)   (fiery, flammable)

If these words were listed in alphabetical order, which word would come **fourth**? Write the answer on the line.

Example kite   colourful   breeze   blow   chase   ___colourful___

6. Earth   Mercury   Venus   Mars   Pluto   _____
7. Paris   London   Prague   Lisbon   Edinburgh   _____
8. bracelet   ring   jewel   bead   bangle   _____
9. silver   red   rouge   gold   ruby   _____
10. ten   two   one   nine   twenty   _____

Using the alphabet to help you, crack the code. You might need to use a different method from the example given. Write your answer on the line.

A B C D E F G H I J K L M N O P Q R S T U V W X Y Z

Example If the code for **CART** is **EZTS**, what is the code for **KING**?   ___MHPF___   (+2, −1, +2, −1)

11. If the code for **SPEAK** is **UPGAM**, what does the code **ILCSUEU** mean? _____
12. If **CUSHION** is written in code as **DWVLNUU**, what is the code for **CHEEKS**? _____
13. If the code **TODKT** means **SOCKS**, what does the code **UIHHUS** mean? _____
14. If **MASK** is written in code as **LZRJ**, what is the code for **CIRCUS**? _____

Work out the answers. Write your answers on the lines.

15. Louise's mum will be twice Louise's age on Louise's next birthday. If Louise's mum will be 44 on Louise's next birthday, how old is Louise now? _____
16. Maya's friend, Nerita, is 17 days older than her. If Maya's birthday is 28 September, when is Nerita's birthday? _____

Score: Time taken: Target met?

Verbal Reasoning Rapid Tests 4   33

Section 3 Test 7

Target time: **10 minutes**

Each word below can be changed into a new word by putting another word in **front**. The added word must be the **same** for each word in the row. Find the word and write it on the line.

Example bow   drop   storm   coat   _____rain_____

1. all   come   see   hear   _____
2. age   card   code   men   _____
3. strict   cave   done   firm   _____
4. not   did   dour   died   _____
5. gain   maid   rage   king   _____

Find **one** missing letter that completes **both** pairs of words. Write it on the lines.

Example tre [_e_] asy   lik [_e_] ver   (tree and easy, like and ever)

6. thre [__] xpect   pan [__] vent   9. vee [__] ange   clea [__] emark
7. sk [__] elp   fra [__] olk   10. san [__] ark   drea [__] odge
8. soo [__] ought   blow [__] asty

Find the **four-letter word** hidden across two or more consecutive words in each sentence below. The order of the letters must stay the same. Underline the word and write it on the line.

Example You certainly <u>do l</u>ead an interesting life.   _____dole_____

11. The athlete was very fit.   _____
12. The businessmen made a deal.   _____
13. Why do you want to be a nurse?   _____
14. Jack is sensible enough to walk to school by himself.   _____

Work out the answers. Write your answers on the lines.

15. Hannah is training for a race. On the first day of her training, she runs for 1 hour. Every day she runs for 5 minutes longer. That means on the second day of training she runs for 1 hour and 5 minutes, on the third day she runs for 1 hour and 10 minutes and so on. For how long will she run on the ninth day of her training?   _____

16. It takes Hayden 120 minutes to organise his stationery. If he begins at 6.15 p.m., at what time will he finish the job?   _____

Score: Time taken: Target met?

Section 3 Test 8

Target time: 10 minutes

Work out the missing number and write it on the line.

Example 36 [6] 6   45 [9] 5   25 [__5__] 5
(a ÷ b = ?, where a represents the number on the left and b represents the number on the right)

1. 66 [11] 6   60 [30] 2   200 [_____] 4
2. 7 [13] 3   4 [12] 4   10 [_____] 2
3. 10 [22] 2   12 [25] 1   5 [_____] 3
4. 12 [16] 3   7 [11] 3   6 [_____] 5
5. 20 [17] 2   10 [4] 5   20 [_____] 4

Underline the two words, **one** from each group, that are most **opposite** in meaning.

Example (<u>agitated</u>, tiger, peace)   (<u>calm</u>, vague, eager)

6. (airport, home, dull)   (abroad, holiday, foreign)
7. (adorn, dislike, adore)   (rude, unfriendly, hate)
8. (sharp, point, poke)   (bleed, blunt, blend)
9. (frail, friend, doe)   (deer, companion, foe)
10. (celebrate, frail, famous)   (unknown, usual, odd)

Change the first word into the last word by changing only **one** letter at a time, making a new word in the middle. Write the new word on the line.

Example LAKE [__LANE__] PANE

11. REAR [_____] FEAT
12. SINK [_____] BUNK
13. RING [_____] GANG
14. KIND [_____] WINE

Work out the answers. Write your answers on the lines.

15. Jo has 2 pairs of red socks, 3 pairs of black socks, 2 pairs of blue socks and an odd pink sock. One of the red pairs and one of the blue pairs are spotty. Twice as many socks have stripes on them. The rest are plain. How many socks are plain? _____

16. In Gerald's class, there are 12 boys and 14 girls. Half the girls have brown hair – 2 more than the boys; 8 children have blonde hair; 2 boys have ginger hair and the rest of the children have black hair. If 5 of the blonde-haired children are girls, how many boys have black hair? _____

Score:	Time taken:	Target met?

Verbal Reasoning Rapid Tests 4

Section 3 Test 9

Target time: 10 minutes

Underline the word that goes best with the three words in brackets.

Example (paint, chalk, pastel)   <u>ink,</u> sketch, colour

1. (noise, din, clamour)   racket, tennis, daze
2. (advice, guidance, counsel)   map, direction, compass
3. (practice, routine, habit)   rehearsal, shop, custom
4. (understanding, deal, agreement)   arrangement, comprehend, continue
5. (worry, anxiety, unease)   confuse, concert, concern

Underline the two words, **one** from each group, that will complete the sentence in the best way.

Example **Detective** is to (inspector, crime, <u>investigate</u>) as **tutor** is to (acrobatics, <u>teach,</u> expect).

6. **Fox** is to (den, hound, chicken) as **badger** is to (pack, sett, tribe).
7. **River** is to (rush, stream, pebble) as **lake** is to (pond, ocean, shore).
8. **Bean** is to (green, been, bane) as **seam** is to (seen, seat, seem).
9. **Drive** is to (dive, engine, drove) as **sleep** is to (sled, rest, slept).
10. **Spade** is to (silt, garden, dig) as **hammer** is to (tool, builder, hammer).

Make a new word by changing the first word of the third pair in the same way as the other pairs. Write the new word on the line.

Example wider, weir   waver, wear   fault, _____flat_____   (take the 1st, 4th, 2nd, 5th letters)

11. lagged, glad   hiccup, chip   online, _____
12. hearth, heat   folder, role   rowing, _____
13. castle, last   pastel, east   watery, _____
14. stride, side   beside, bide   rewind, _____

Work out the answers. Write your answers on the lines.

15. Gillian is 4 months older than her friend Susan. If Gillian's birthday is in December, when is Susan's birthday? _____
16. Lucas is going on holiday for a fortnight on 10 July. What date will he return? _____

Section 3 Test 10

Target time: 10 minutes

Use the information given to answer the sum. Write your answer as a **letter**.

Example A = 15   B = 29   C = 32   D = 60   E = 8   **D ÷ A × E =** __C__   (60 ÷ 15 × 8 = 32)

1. A = 40   B = 2   C = 24   D = 4   E = 26   **A ÷ B + D =** _____
2. A = 100   B = 25   C = 5   D = 70   E = 71   **A − B − C =** _____
3. A = 11   B = 88   C = 3   D = 8   E = 14   **B ÷ A + C =** _____
4. A = 23   B = 26   C = 0   D = 4   E = 3   **E + A − B =** _____
5. A = 44   B = 2   C = 64   D = 12   E = 24   **C ÷ B + D =** _____

In each group, three words go together and two are the odd ones out. Underline the **two** words that do **not** go with the other three.

Example scalding, sweltering, <u>bitter</u>, <u>raw</u>, roasting

6. balance, lean, slim, slender, incline
7. fair, just, fare, equal, bill
8. merry, jolly, bland, brash, cheerful
9. scale, fish, climb, mount, capture
10. exclaim, yell, outrage, bellow, shock

Using the alphabet to help you, find the letters that complete each sentence. Write the letters on the line. You might need to use a different method from the example given.

A B C D E F G H I J K L M N O P Q R S T U V W X Y Z

Example **JB** is to **PY** as **KR** is to __QO__.   (+6, −3)

11. **YB** is to **BA** as **CV** is to _____.
12. **BQ** is to **XT** as **WX** is to _____.
13. **YZ** is to **DX** as **HA** is to _____.
14. **IC** is to **RX** as **UP** is to _____.

Work out the answers. Write your answers on the lines.

15. Mr and Mrs Bright are having a new carpet fitted. Mrs Bright measures the room. It is 5.5m wide and 6.5m long. The carpet is supplied in tiles that measure 1m². How many carpet tiles will they need to completely cover the floor? _____

16. Giles bought new trainers in the sale. They were reduced by 25% to £30. How much did Giles save? _____

Score: Time taken: Target met?

Verbal Reasoning Rapid Tests 4   37

Section 3 Test 11

Target time: 10 minutes

Underline the two words, **one** from each group, that will complete the sentence in the best way.

Example **Detective** is to (inspector, crime, <u>investigate</u>) as **tutor** is to (acrobatics, <u>teach,</u> expect).

1. **Trip** is to (part, trap, kerb) as **swim** is to (mews, swam, stroke).
2. **Eight** is to (count, spider, ate) as **four** is to (lose, for, snake).
3. **Blind** is to (peek, site, sight) as **deaf** is to (heard, hearing, listen).
4. **Help** is to (assist, impair, injured) as **damage** is to (bandage, upset, harm).
5. **Frog** is to (pond, flies, tadpole) as **sheep** is to (grass, fence, calf).

Find the missing number in the sequence. Write it on the line.

Example 32   28   20   16   8   __4__   (repeating pattern −4, −8)

6. 21   28   35   42   49   _____
7. 200   400   _____   1600   3200
8. 48   27   24   9   12   3   _____   1
9. 10   7   14   11   _____   19   38
10. 80   40   36   18   14   _____

Find **one** missing letter that completes **both** pairs of words. Write it on the lines.

Example tre [_e_] asy   lik [_e_] ver   (tree and easy, like and ever)

11. shel [__] igure   scar [__] ight   13. lis [__] ause   tuli [__] each
12. entic [__] xact   eras [__] nact   14. mot [__] int   fift [__] oney

Work out the answers. Write your answers on the lines.

15. Selina collects buttons. She has 32 large, 24 medium and 31 small buttons. Half of the large buttons have 2 holes and a quarter of them have 4 holes. All except 3 of the medium buttons have 4 holes and 12 of the small buttons have 2 holes. The rest of the buttons have 1 hole. How many buttons have 4 holes? _____

16. Ollie and his 7 friends are having their school lunch. 2 of the friends have sausages and mash, 4 of them have pizza and chips and the others have a chicken salad. Half the children eating pizza and chips have sponge and custard for dessert; the rest of the children have a piece of fruit. All the children eating chicken salad have water to drink and the rest drink juice. How many children drink juice? _____

Score: _____   Time taken: _____   Target met? _____

Section 3 Test 12

Target time: 10 minutes

Find the missing number in each equation. Write the number on the line.

Example 72 + 3 = 25 × ___3___   (72 + 3 = 75 and so does 25 × 3)

1. 17 + 3 = 15 + 4 + _____
2. 77 ÷ 11 = 15 − _____
3. 42 ÷ 7 = 3 × _____
4. 51 + 5 = 7 × _____
5. 44 ÷ 4 = 10 + _____

Underline the pair of words that are most **opposite** in meaning.

Example (<u>agitated, calm</u>)   (peace, vague)   (tiger, eager)

6. (curious, content)   (continue, cease)   (ease, canvas)
7. (reveal, hide)   (trick, mask)   (forget, recite)
8. (sold, cell)   (always, after)   (seldom, often)
9. (establish, economy)   (permanent, temporary)   (decide, forgive)
10. (open, secretive)   (joyful, cheerful)   (perform, peruse)

Match the number codes to the words. One code is missing. Use these to work out the answers to the questions. Write your answers on the lines.

CHIP   CHAT   PEAK   CHAP   5869   4167   4165

11–13. What is the code for: **PATCH**? _____   **PEACE**? _____   **CHEAT**? _____

14. What does the code **58641** mean? _____

Choose the **true** statements from the selection below. Circle the letter next to those statements.

15–16. Triangles are 2D shapes with three sides. An isosceles triangle is a type of triangle.

If the above statements are true, which **two** of the following statements must also be true? Circle the **two** correct answers.

A An isosceles triangle has three sides.
B Isosceles triangles are 2D shapes.
C Squares are bigger than triangles.
D An isosceles triangle contains two right angles.

Progress chart

Write the score (out of 16) for each test in the box provided on the right of the graph.
Then colour in the row next to the box to represent this score.

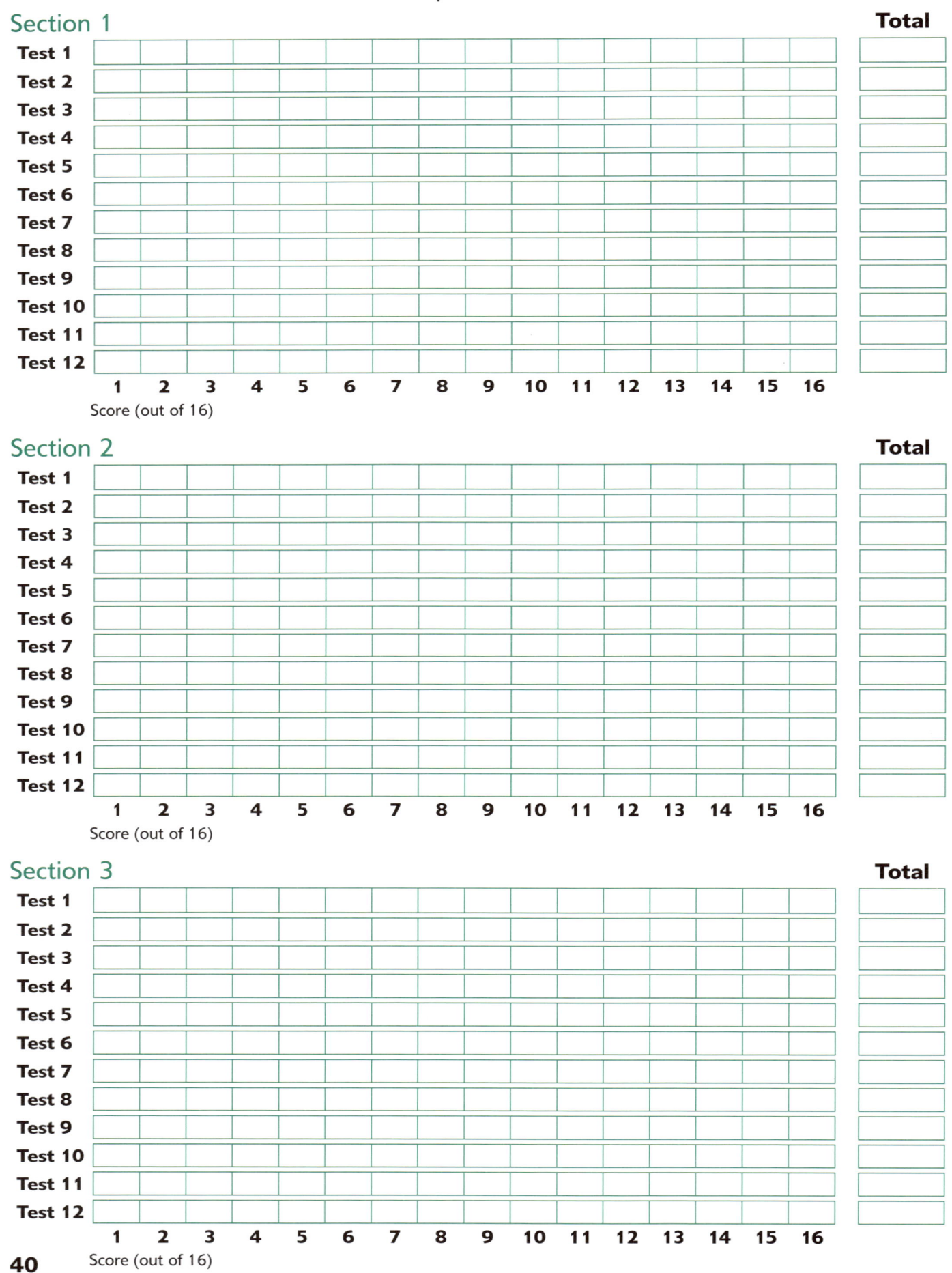

Section 1 — Total

Test 1
Test 2
Test 3
Test 4
Test 5
Test 6
Test 7
Test 8
Test 9
Test 10
Test 11
Test 12

Score (out of 16): 1 2 3 4 5 6 7 8 9 10 11 12 13 14 15 16

Section 2 — Total

Test 1
Test 2
Test 3
Test 4
Test 5
Test 6
Test 7
Test 8
Test 9
Test 10
Test 11
Test 12

Score (out of 16): 1 2 3 4 5 6 7 8 9 10 11 12 13 14 15 16

Section 3 — Total

Test 1
Test 2
Test 3
Test 4
Test 5
Test 6
Test 7
Test 8
Test 9
Test 10
Test 11
Test 12

Score (out of 16): 1 2 3 4 5 6 7 8 9 10 11 12 13 14 15 16